Landscapes

MARGARET WILLES

The National Trust

First published in Great Britain in 1999 by
National Trust Enterprises Ltd
36 Queen Anne's Gate, London SW1H 9AS
http://bookshelf.nationaltrust.org.uk

British Library Cataloguing in Publication Data
A catalogue record for this book is available from the British Library.

ISBN 0 7078 0345 4

Picture research by Margaret Willes
Designed and typeset by Peter and Alison Guy
Production by Dee Maple
Print managed by Centurion Press Ltd (HGP)

Front cover: *The medieval ruins of Corfe Castle, Dorset, rising through the mist.*
Title page: *Statue of the River God by John Cheere in the cave of the Grotto
at Stourhead Landscape Garden, Wiltshire.*
Back cover: *View across Derwentwater, Cumbria.*

Introduction

This book was born out of the research that I undertook for the National Trust Desk Diary for the year 2000. It seemed appropriate that such a momentous date should be commemorated by considerations of time, and so I took various landscapes and looked at the way time had wrought changes on them. Several of those landscapes are here, along with others which appealed to me as I warmed to my theme.

What exactly is a landscape? According to the Oxford English Dictionary, the earliest use of the word in English, in the late sixteenth century, was adopted from a Dutch painter's term, *landskip*. Only later does it develop the meaning of a view of the countryside which we use much more commonly. The original connection with painting is important. Henry Hoare's superb landscape garden at Stourhead in Wiltshire, laid out in the 1740s and 50s, was designed to conjure up an Arcadian vision, idealised in the paintings of Claude Lorraine and Nicholas Poussin. Travellers visiting the Lake District in the 1760s and 70s carried special convex mirrors in their baggage so that they might enjoy the magnificent landscapes through the eyes of Claude Lorraine.

Many of the landscapes mentioned have been shaped over long periods of time. The extraordinary structure of the Giant's Causeway on the Antrim coast of Northern Ireland was the result of thousands of years of volcanic activity. But landscapes can alter quite quickly too, especially on the coast. The coal-blackened coastline of Durham, for instance, has changed quite radically in less than ten years. That change has been effected by the hand of man, and most of the landscapes included here are in some degree or other the creation of man, such as the 'floating' water meadows at Sherborne in Gloucestershire.

Encapsulating a vast subject in such a short text has been incredibly difficult. This is merely a taster of some of the magnificent landscapes to be seen in England, Wales and Northern Ireland, many of them in the care of the National Trust. My colleagues have been very generous in providing information and great days out. I would like to thank the following for their help: Steve Judd, Adrian Colston, Chris Gingell, Jon Brookes, Paul Boland, Peter Katic, Alison Fawcett, Jonathan Fisher, Dennis Rooney, Angus Wainwright, Mary Salter, David Adshead, David Thackray, Rob Woodside, Andy Mayled, Hilary Moorcroft, Richard Offen and Adrian Tinniswood.

Avebury

Avebury in Wiltshire is the most important Neolithic site in Britain, a complex of various monuments and earthworks used as a focus for ceremonial activities as long ago as 3700 BC. It lies only twenty miles from Stonehenge, but in a very different landscape. While the great circle of Stonehenge stands isolated on a chalk plateau of Salisbury Plain, Avebury is located at the headwater of the River Kennet, lying in much more fertile and welcoming surroundings.

The complex is bewildering to read from the ground, including long barrows such as West Kennet; a causewayed enclosure on Windmill Hill; stone circles and the remains of wooden ones on Overton Hill – the 'Sanctuary'; a huge earthwork rising from the valley floor at Silbury Hill; and the stone circles or henge at Avebury itself, with an avenue of stones leading from there to the Sanctuary. Attracted by the fertility of the area and easy access to good communication routes such as the ancient path of the Ridgeway, communities have inhabited the landscape around Avebury down through the centuries. But the spiritual power continued too: in the Middle Ages, when a village was established just outside the Avebury henge, superstitious villagers tried to bury some of the stones.

Although mentioned in passing by topographical writers, Avebury's rediscovery as a historical site came in 1648 when John Aubrey was out hunting. A keen antiquarian, he was familiar with Stonehenge, but the stones and mighty bank at Avebury astounded him: indeed he likened it to a cathedral, while Stonehenge was a parish church. He was to be fascinated by his 'cathedral' for the rest of his life, observing and drawing.

Influenced by his reading of Roman writers, Aubrey identified Avebury as a Druid temple. A later interpretation by William Stukeley expanded on this theme: the monuments, he decided, formed the outline of a great serpent, a result of the association of Druid rites with Egyptian hieroglyphics. Archaeological excavation has disproved the more exotic theories, but shown that Avebury was indeed a site of supreme ceremonial importance. For many, it continues to be so.

Upper Wharfedale

Upper Wharfedale lies in the north-western part of the Yorkshire Dales, running from Bolton Abbey up to Langstrothdale, and providing a landscape of outstanding beauty. Dale is the Viking word for valley, and these dales were carved out of the Pennines by glaciers. As the rock is largely limestone, there are no lakes, but rivers and waterfalls that tumble fiercely after rain, and are reduced to a gentle trickle in the dry seasons.

For millennia this has been an agricultural landscape, with generations of farmers leaving their mark upon the countryside. At Grassington, when the sun casts long shadows, the ghostly form of Iron Age field banks or lynchets come into focus. In Upper Wharfedale, the Dark Ages were probably not so dark: grazing and cropping were the order of the day rather than rape and pillage. By 866 Ivan the Boneless had sailed up the Ouse with his Danes and taken York. The Norwegians meanwhile had crossed from Ireland and the Orkneys to Cumbria, and both groups met and integrated with the indigenous folk of the Dales.

The rich mixture of place names reflect this: Wharfe itself is the name of a Celtic goddess, Hubberholme comes from the Old English for Hunburg's homestead, while Yockenthwaite is the thwaite – Danish for clearing – of the Celt, Eogan. Place names give the clue to Wharfedale's later communities, too. When rebellion broke out in this region not long after the Norman Conquest, William I carried out a scorched earth policy known as the Harrying of the North. Farmers continued to cultivate their strips of land, but under the feudal government of the king's leading supporters. Areas specifically for hunting deer and boar were set aside – Royal Forests for the king, chases for his nobles. Langstrothdale was held by the Percy earls of Northumberland, who housed their foresters at the appropriately named Buckden.

The third element in the medieval landscape of the Dales was the monastic granges, large sheep farms controlled by religious houses. Perhaps the greatest farmers of all were the Cistercian monks from Fountains Abbey, whose headquarters were at Kilnsey, astride Mastiles Lane, the main route to Cumbria. Kilnsey itself means the kiln in the marsh, a reminder that lime was burnt and scattered to counteract the natural leaching of the soil.

Despite all their power and wealth, the great landowners and the monks were not to prove the enduring element of Upper Wharfedale – late medieval politics and the Dissolution of the Monasteries put paid to this. Instead, small farmers created the landscape that we see today, moderately sized fields enclosed by dry-stone walls. At first these enclosures of previously common land – intakes – were unofficial and irregular in shape, their sites midway up the valley slopes. Later enclosures were the result of Acts of Parliament, and these are very regular, with walls as straight as a die, swooping down the fellside.

Yockenthwaite provides a good example of a traditional Wharfedale farming community. A hamlet rather than a village, it is approached by a narrow packhorse bridge over the River Wharfe, and lies in the shelter of a sycamore belt. Once there were six farms, now it has only two, their eighteenth-century farmhouses with handsome Georgian doorcases and sash windows. Yockenthwaite Cottage still has the older, mullion windows.

In the fields around Yockenthwaite are the characteristic barns of the area, of local stone with lintels and copings of millstone grit. Cattle were traditionally overwintered on the lower level, in stalls separated by slate boskins, while a ceiling of woven hazel supported the hay in the level above. The hay meadows were cut in July and the cattle allowed to graze until winter, when they were taken into the field barns. In spring, the manure collected from the midden, a small enclosure adjacent to the barn, was spread onto the fields. The National Trust now owns nine of these farms – in 1988 Graham Watson presented eight of them, and the following year Laura Mason bequeathed the ninth. Here the Trust continues the process of low intensity management, with the farmers receiving grants to manage and maintain the unique landscape. The hay meadows are cut late to encourage wild flowers such as yellow-rattle, eyebright and burnt saxifrage to flourish.

Yockenthwaite on the banks of the River Wharfe.

West Penwith

The ancient field landscape of West Penwith, looking from Carn Galver towards the sea.

West Penwith is a rectangle of land stretching along the north coast of Cornwall from the seaside town of St Ives westwards to Lands End. To one side the granite moorland rises to dramatic carns, on the other lie rocky headlands and coves with farms surrounded by small, stone-hedged fields, narrow lanes and here and there the remains of engine houses. This is a countryside of intense beauty, but it is also, according to archaeologists, the oldest working landscape in the world.

At Rosemergy Farm, for instance, can be seen the form of an Iron Age farm. Three thousand years ago, when the climate was slightly warmer, farmers cleared small fields radiating out from their farm-steads, dividing them with Cornish hedges – walls of stone infilled by rubble and soil – and lynchets or terraces were formed to cope with the slope towards the sea. Here they grew barley and wheat, raised cattle and sheep, moving from field to field as the soil was exhausted. Forts were built on headlands such as Bosigran and Gurnard. Bosigran means 'farm of igran', said to be the home of Ygran, mother of King Arthur. Within the fort's defences there are no remains of a settlement, suggesting it might have been neutral ground where trading could take place. Gurnard Head, on the other hand, has hut circles of stone.

Iron Age huts gave way to Romano-Cornish houses built around courtyards and strung along streets, then to medieval farmsteads, as this land was constantly in cultivation. The sea too contributed to this precarious existence. From the late eighteenth century, the main catch was pilchards, known locally as fair maids, probably a corruption of the Spanish word for smoked, *fumadoe*. The arrival of vast shoals, flashing silver in the water, would cause all other activities to cease. A huer, stationed on the headland, would use a branch of gorse to signal to his companions in their boats, indicating where the shoals lay beneath them. The catch was then packed into hogsheads on the shore, loaded into ships bound for the Mediterranean countries where pilchards were appreciated on days of abstinence from meat. The pilchards' final departure was as dramatic as their arrivals – the industry died in the early 1900s as a result of over-fishing.

The engine houses and chimneys that punctuate the landscape of West Penwith are reminders of the area's third industry, tin mining. At Porthmoina the original, eighteenth-century mining was surface. Later, shafts were dug and engine houses erected for winding gear. The stone came up to be broken into fist-sized pieces by local women, known as bal maidens, before descending through stamping machines and a series of pools gradually to refine the tin ore. The ore was then taken to Hayle, where tin's faithful companion, arsenic, was burned off and exported to the United States to kill off the boll weevil preying on the cotton fields.

Porthmoina has now reverted to a rural landscape, the remains of mine works cloaked in undergrowth. But travel further west to St Just and Cape Cornwall, and mining dominates the landscape: terraces of miner's cottages, engine houses and chimneys are everywhere. The boom time here was the late nineteenth century, when St Just suddenly became a town. The mines were usually owned by co-operatives, financed by investors. At Botallack the Count House is being restored by the National Trust. On the ground floor were the administrative offices of the mine, above, a banqueting room where the investors could be wined and dined. Close by is the Botallack Mine Set, including a magnificent building reminiscent of a Roman basilica. An arched flue ran like a snake through this building from the burning house to the chimney to provide the draw. To keep the draw effective, miners had to scrape the arsenic from the walls.

Reminders of the harshness of miners' lives are constant. Many had to walk several miles to reach the pits, climb down the shafts by ladder – sometimes to below sea level, and then walk another couple of miles to the face. Their traditional meal was a Cornish pasty – the filling was eaten, but the pastry case thrown away because their hands were covered in arsenic. In the late nineteenth century the average age of these miners was twenty-seven. Even then, there was not enough employment and thousands left to work in mines in Africa, America and Australia: it was said that if you shouted down a hole in the ground anywhere in the world, a Cornishman would reply. But now the last of the Penwith mines, Geevor, has closed, bringing this long and often tragic chapter to an end.

[12]

The mouth of the Kenidjack Valley at St Just, with the great wheelpit of Wheal Call on the right, and the pumping engine house in the background.

The White Cliffs of Dover

The chalk cliffs of Dover represent one of the symbolic landscapes of Britain. Here the North Downs run down to the English Channel, the cliffs formed from the fossilised remains of myriads of microscopic sea creatures which settled at the bottom of the ocean over a hundred million years ago. In sunlight the cliffs are a brilliant white – sharp-eyed Romans looking out from the shores of Gaul noted them and called the mysterious island Albion from *alba*, Latin for white. When shrouded in misty rain the cliffs can look a wan grey, while sunrise and sunset imbue them with a golden glow.

This south-east corner of Kent is only twenty miles from the French coast, the narrowest point between the British Isles and mainland Europe. For those who came to conquer, the White Cliffs represented Britain's first line of defence, so William the Conqueror built a castle here soon after his victory at Hastings in 1066. In the Second World War, tunnels dug through the yielding chalk below the castle provided shelter for troops and civilians when this part of the coast, known as Hellfire Corner, came under fire from German artillery.

For returning travellers, the White Cliffs were a sign that they were home – providing they could cope with the notorious banks of the Goodwin Sands. Dubbed the 'Great Ship Swallower', they have proved disastrous for many vessels, as can be seen on the beach below Langdon Cliffs, where lies the wreck of the *Preussan*, a sailing ship run aground in 1910. The Romans erected two lighthouses or *pharos*; one still survives within Dover Castle. Sixteen hundred years later, South Foreland Lighthouse was built specifically to help sailors navigate the Goodwins. Originally lit by oil, it later became the first electrically powered lighthouse in the British Isles. But once out of sight of land, ships were still entirely isolated until Marconi carried out the first ship-to-shore demonstration of radio transmission from South Foreland to the East Goodwin lightship, a distance of twelve miles. This took place in foul weather over Christmas and New Year 1898, celebrated by Marconi's assistant, G.S. Kemp, with a prolonged bout of seasickness aboard the lightship.

Hatfield Forest

'The only place where one can step back into the Middle Ages to see, with only a small effort of the imagination, what a Forest looked like in use.' Thus Oliver Rackham introduces Hatfield Forest, one and a half square miles of wild landscape in north-west Essex, in *The Last Forest*.

The idea of a Royal Forest came to England in the eleventh century with William the Conqueror. An area of rough land where the king or one of his magnates had the right to keep deer, to kill and to eat them, the Forest was not necessarily a place of trees: some of the Norman Forests were on fenland, others on moorland. Hatfield was – and is – a mixture of woodland areas with native oak, hornbeam and hazel, and open, grassy chases. In the woodland the trees were coppiced – cut right down so that the stump might send up shoots from which the wood could be harvested. Forests were never exclusively a hunting preserve, and the local farmers also grazed their animals here. To protect the coppices, woodbanks were built around the trees, while those in the chases were pollarded, their tops cut but with plenty of trunk left to protect them.

[16]

In Hatfield the Forest Laws prevailed – these were known as *venison* and *vert*, and protected the two vital elements of the landscape. Venison was the meat of the fallow deer introduced by the Normans, and so valued that it was never sold on the open market. Vert, or green, represented the trees, again a valuable product for the Crown. Tradition says the Laws were savage, but records show that revenue from fines rather than violent punishment was the order of the day.

Hatfield Forest survived because it was bought in the early eighteenth century by the Houblon family, who made some changes to provide a picturesque landscape, such as draining the heavy clay to create a lake and building a fashionable shell house on its bank, but for the rest continued to maintain grazing and coppicing. The Forest is now looked after by the National Trust who have revived these traditional practices and provide not only an ancient landscape but also a sanctuary for flora and fauna, including the old quarry of the Norman kings, the fallow deer.

The Isle of Purbeck

The ruins of Corfe Castle in Dorset are set dramatically on a steep hill, with the village clinging around their base. It is a curiously un-English sight, much more like the *bastides* to be found in the great valleys of southern France. Perhaps this is not entirely a conceit, for Corfe was one of the favourite castles of King John, with an Angevin father and a mother from Aquitaine.

The castle stands on a mound that forms part of the main chalk ridge running east to west across the Isle of Purbeck, on the south Dorset coast. Two rivers cut through the ridge, creating the mound – the name Corfe is derived from the Old English for a gap or cutting. The present castle was begun by William the Conqueror, quick to recognise the strategic value of such a site, though archaeological evidence suggests the presence of an earlier, Anglo-Saxon palace. Legend supports this, for Corfe is said to be the site of royal murder most foul, on 18 March 978 when Edward, King of Wessex and all England, was struck down by his stepmother, Elfrida, who wanted to put her own son Ethelred on the throne. Edward passed into history as the Martyr King, while his half-brother was dubbed Ethelred the Unready, and the first Weak King of England according to *1066 And All That*.

King John, described by the same source as Awful, was forced to cede Normandy to his French cousin, making the south of England his vulnerable front line. Corfe was strengthened by building a deep ditch between the castle and the village, and new domestic quarters, known as the Gloriette, were constructed. Here the king's niece, the damsel of Brittany, was imprisoned in some style, while her unfortunate knights were starved to death in a dungeon called Butavant. King John did nothing by halves. The castle survived intact until the seventeenth-century Civil War when it was slighted to prevent it being used in war again. Even then, the medieval work was so good that considerable remains survived to create a fashionably romantic ruin.

The ruins of the medieval Corfe Castle that form the gateway to the Isle of Purbeck.

The sun setting on St Aldhelm's Head on the southerly tip of the Isle of Purbeck. This is a highly worked landscape, with the limestone quarried and shipped out for cathedrals and palaces.

From Corfe Castle fine views can be had over the landscape of the Isle of Purbeck – not an island at all, but a peninsula, roughly rectangular in shape, ten miles long by seven wide. It is quite geologically diverse, the layers running east to west like stripes in Neapolitan ice cream, and this diversity gives Purbeck a richness both of natural history and of landscape.

The most northerly part of the Isle is made up of a layer of grits and gravels yielding lowland heath. Here King John was able to indulge his passion for hunting deer and boar, but now the surviving heathland provides habitats for British reptiles and birds including Dartford warblers and the hobby. The next layer is the chalk ridge on which Corfe Castle stands. Immediately south of the village is an area of fen and damp grassland, formerly common land and therefore never ploughed. Rich grassland flora such as marsh-orchid, adders-tongue fern and green-winged orchid flourish here. The third layer is of Wealden clay, providing fertile farmland for generations of settlers.

South again, and the rock becomes limestone, yielding the marbles of Purbeck and Portland stone. The latter was extracted right on the coast around Seaham and St Aldhelm's Head, where the cliff quarries are supported by pillars, giving them an architectural quality. In the seventeenth century, this stone was dressed on shore and sent to London to rebuild the City churches and St Paul's Cathedral after the Great Fire of 1666.

Purbeck marble comes from two seams of hard limestone, one grey-green, the other red. It has been quarried since Roman times, but became internationally famous in the Middle Ages when the Crusaders returned from the Holy Land with a taste for marble. In this case the stone was not dressed at the quarries, or quarrs, but taken by hollow ways up to the village of Corfe Castle to be shaped before shipping to various parts of England, Normandy, and even to Italy. Purbeck marble can be seen in some of England's greatest cathedrals, including Canterbury, Winchester and Westminster. Perhaps the ultimate accolade, however, must be the effigy of King John in Worcester Cathedral, made in his favourite Isle of Purbeck.

The Giant's Causeway

Detail from one of the gouaches of the Giant's Causeway, painted by Susanna Drury in 1740, showing some of the earliest tourists to the site.

The Giant's Causeway is one of the most spectacular features of the Antrim coast of Northern Ireland. It was formed sixty million years ago when volcanic activity caused the earlier chalk landscape to be covered by layers of lava. This surface began to weather, creating a layer of soil which now shows as a red seam. On top came another layer of lava which lost its heat slowly and evenly, creating regular cracks like drying mud, and cracking vertically too, to produce polygonal columns that now look so strange and man made. In all there are 40,000 of these columns on the Irish coast, with a similar formation on the Scottish island of Staffa. Little wonder that legends grew up about giants building the causeway to fight each other, and then tearing it up again.

Although inhabited since prehistoric times, the Causeway was cut off from the rest of the world, not even making its appearance on the map of Ireland until 1714. It was the Royal Society, incorporated by Charles II to discuss 'new or experimental philosophy', that brought the Giant's Causeway to the eyes of the world. A paper by Dr Samuel Foley, Bishop of Down and Connor, was published in 1694, instituting a scientific debate about the geological formation of the Causeway that ran for nearly a century and seemed particularly to appeal to churchmen.

The protagonists divided themselves into the Neptunists and the Vulcanists. Neptunists believed that particles in the seawater had settled on the seabed and become first mud, then columns. Vulcanists plumped for a volcanic origin. In 1740 Susanna Drury, a little known artist from Dublin, spent three months on site to produce two paintings. They provided at last an accurate image, but confused as well as informed because some Vulcanists put her prospects side by side and deduced a mountain in the middle from which lava flowed. The mystery was finally solved in 1786 when Dr William Hamilton, Rector of Clondevadock in Donegal, concluded correctly that the Causeway was part of a larger volcanic area.

Susanna Drury's two paintings of the Giant's Causeway were made into engravings by François Vivares and distributed all over Britain and Europe, turning the Causeway into a major tourist attraction. A road down to the stones had been built in the late seventeenth century, but it was frequently impassable and visitors had therefore to leave their carriages on the cliff top and make their way down on foot, or approach by boat. The novelist William Makepeace Thackeray paid a visit in 1842, but his woes could be echoed by many a visitor to popular tourist sites today: 'Mon Dieu, and have I travelled 150 miles to see that! The guides pounce upon the visitor, with a dozen rough boatmen who are lying in wait … I had no friends: I was perfectly helpless … Four men seized a boat, pushed it into the water, and ravished me into it.'

Local inhabitants were quick to see the commercial potential. They combined fishing and burning seaweed with duties as guides and sellers of fossils and crystals. Thackeray describes one such, Old Mary, who sold whiskey and water from a wishing well on the Little Causeway. 'Did you serve old Saturn with a glass when he lay along the Causeway here?' he asked. 'In reply she says she has no change for a shilling; she never has: but her whisky is good.'

In 1855 the Belfast to Portrush railway was opened, bringing tourists within seven miles of the Causeway. They could then complete their journey by jaunting-car. Two hotels were built close by. One, the Causeway, offered hot and cold showers, 'Comfortable Cars with Careful Drivers always in Readiness, Good boats and Practical Boatmen.' The final piece in the jigsaw of access was the hydroelectric tramway, first of its kind, linking Portrush and Bushmills in 1883. Although intended to transport heavy goods, it also brought visitors *en masse* – in 1887, for instance, 62,000 came by tramline and rush hour, when everybody wanted to get out, proved a hair-raising experience. The rise in numbers continued, so that when the National Trust took over the Giant's Causeway in 1961, one of its principal tasks was to balance access to the stones with protecting the natural habitats from damage by the feet of visitors, currently running at over half a million each year.

Sunset over some of the basalt columns of the Giant's Causeway.

Stourhead Landscape Garden

A view of the garden at Stourhead, with the Temple of Apollo, the Palladian Bridge and the Pantheon, a watercolour by Coplestone Warre Bampfylde, painted in 1775. Visitors are taking the circuit path over the bridge and around the lake.

Stourhead lives up to its name – the source of the River Stour, lying on the western scarp of the chalklands of Wessex. In medieval times the valley was owned by the Stourton family, who secured a licence in 1448 to make it into a park. As lords of the springs of the Stour they even included six fountains in their coat of arms.

The estate was bought in 1717 by the banker, Henry Hoare I, who pulled down the Tudor mansion of the Stourtons, building instead a grand villa in the newly fashionable Palladian style to the designs of Colen Campbell, and renamed it Stourhead. Hardly had he completed the house when he died, leaving his widow a life interest in the estate; thereafter it would pass to his son, also called Henry, and known in the family as 'the Magnificent'.

As a director of Hoare's Bank in London's Fleet Street, Henry Hoare II was a very rich man. His customers included architects such as Sir John Vanbrugh and William Kent, and literary figures like the poets Alexander Pope and John Gay. He also delighted in 'looking into books and the pursuit of that knowledge which distinguishes the Gentleman from the Vulgar', enjoying particularly the works of the Roman poets, Ovid and Virgil. In March 1738 he set off for Italy, taking a Grand Tour that was to last for three years. In Rome he purchased paintings and engravings, many of them landscapes of the Campagna – the Arcadian idyll inhabited by shepherds and classical antiquities. These now form part of the great art collection at Stourhead.

The death of his mother in 1741 brought Henry Hoare back to England. He could now enter his inheritance at Stourhead and develop the landscape. Many cultured Englishmen were creating landscape gardens at this period, based on the ideas of the fifteenth-century Italian humanist, Alberti, whose *Ten Books on Architecture* were first published in an English translation in 1726. He recommended grottoes, caverns, springs, and 'the prospect remains of Antiquity'. Henry Hoare decided that his garden at Stourhead would reflect its history, and be dedicated to the pagan deities of the rivers and springs, and to the Trojan hero, Æneas.

The Palladian Bridge and, beyond, the Pantheon, photographed in the evening light.

The landscape that Henry Hoare had to work on at Stourhead was a valley with two lakes, and he resolved to create a circuit of walks around them. In 1744 he commissioned the architect Henry Flitcroft to build the first of the classical eye-catchers, the Temple of Flora, followed by a grotto in which he placed the statue of Tiber, the River God. His reference here was from Virgil's *Aeneid*: the landing of Aeneas in Italy where he meets Old Tiber. Tiber points towards Hoare's next creation, a Pantheon on the hill above, a reminder that the Pantheon in Rome was said to have been built over Æneas's tomb.

Henry Hoare was a fascinating combination – his garden is full of 'natural beauty' and yet most of the buildings within it are designed in the severe classical style. Unlike Nathaniel Curzon and Robert Adam who swept away the existing village from their ideal landscape at Kedleston in Derbyshire, he chose to retain the ancient village of Stourton with its medieval church, adding a Gothic market cross that he had rescued from Bristol. Legend had it that Alfred the Great had raised his standard at Stourton on his way to defeat the Danes at Edington, and Hoare therefore built Alfred's Tower up on the ridge above Stourhead in 1772. He was making a political point: Alfred had put his country before all things – unlike the first two Hanoverian kings, who embroiled Britain in expensive wars to defend their German interests. Hoare hoped that the new king, George III, would prove a peaceful patriot. Everything linked up in Hoare's fruitful imagination. Æneas's grandson Brutus was, according to the medieval historian Geoffrey of Monmouth, the founder of the British race, and thus ancestor of King Alfred.

From the outset, he intended his garden to be open to visitors, 'the Gentlemen' who would appreciate the cultural associations as they came upon the various buildings and features. But the garden also appealed to 'the Vulgar' who came in huge numbers to enjoy the natural beauty and peace of Stourhead. Mrs Lybbe Powys, an indefatigable tourist, visited in the 1760s and found the Spread Eagle, the inn built by Hoare to accommodate visitors, was full. Undaunted, she returned the next day, declaring both house and garden 'vastly well worth seeing'. Visitors ever since have agreed with this sentiment: the landscape garden at Stourhead is one of the National Trust's most popular properties.

Llanerchaeron

Llanerchaeron lies on the very western seaboard of mainland Britain. A small country estate, it has been the home of generations of Welsh squires ever since Llewelyn Parry bought 500 acres in the valley of the Aeron, close by the Cardigan coast in 1634. Llanerchaeron may be remote, but the family sent their sons to Oxford University, made careers in the Church and the law, and proved remarkably progressive in matters architectural. In 1790, therefore, William Lewis commissioned the fashionable architect John Nash, to provide him with an elegant villa – a working farm in the tradition of ancient Rome and Renaissance Italy. Nash also designed within the picturesque landscape a parish church in the style of a classical temple, and estate cottages in the rustic Gothick style, while the home farm was also either by him or by one of his followers.

William Lewis was a keenly progressive farmer, operating a sort of benevolent agricultural despotism. Tenants had to lime their land, trim their hedges, bring their corn to his mill and rear a hound puppy apiece for his hunting kennels, but he also provided financial support when times were difficult. Wander around Llanerchaeron today, and his orderly spirit hovers. In the rickyard of the home farm stand stone bases, one kind for drying hay, another for corn. In the pleasure ground runs a picturesque stream, a leat from the ornamental pond to provide dipping wells for the gardens and water to sluice out the lavatories and drains. This ingenious combination of the aesthetic and utilitarian runs right through Llanerchaeron.

When the last squire, John Powell Ponsonby Lewes, died in 1989, the National Trust accepted the property despite a lack of funds, because it is such a superb, almost unique, example of a Georgian country estate. A series of schemes has been launched that look to the future not only for the estate, but for the local community too. The repair of the house and ancillary buildings by local craftsmen gives apprentices the chance to train in restoration skills. The home farm and parkland are being converted to organic status, with a flock of local Llanwenog sheep, and the kitchen gardens bustle with life under the care of volunteers who sell their fruit and vegetable crops to visitors.

The Lake District

The area of Cumbria and north Lancashire known as the Lake District is world famous for its picturesque scenery, yet it is a surprisingly small area. During the Ice Ages, snow from domes of old, hard rock, now the peaks of Skiddaw, Helvellyn and Scafell, pushed downwards, packing into glaciers that carved out the steep valleys, and melting into the deep waters that form the lakes. For centuries this landscape was remote and poor. Monasteries such as Fountains Abbey in Yorkshire kept their sheep in granges here, while some valleys were farmed by 'statesmen' or small independent farmers.

The eighteenth century changed all this. When the rebel forces of Charles Stuart, the Young Pretender, managed to penetrate south as far as Derby, the government in London resolved to improve the communication routes to Scotland, and by 1768 a levelled and surfaced road ran north through Westmorland and Cumberland. Where access led, taste followed. In October 1769 the poet Thomas Gray journeyed from Keswick to Lancaster, writing letters to a friend, and with their publication, travellers made their way up to the Lake District in increasing numbers. Like Gray, many carried a Claude Glass in their baggage. This was a slightly convex mirror that enabled the viewer to create an image of the landscape imbued with the atmosphere of the artist Claude Lorraine.

The cult of the Picturesque had taken hold. Its archpriest was the Rev. William Gilpin, Cumbrian born, who defined Picturesque beauty as looking well in a picture, promoting his ideas through a series of books of tours. But he also suggested that it was not necessary for tourists to accept passively what they saw, rather they should develop their experience by using their imagination. This idea had already been taken up by Thomas West in his *Guide to the Lakes* where he recommended stations for the best views. Claife Station overlooking Windermere is now a ruin, but in the late eighteenth century it was an octagonal tower with an upper room furnished with chairs, a fireplace, an aeolian harp and three large windows, each bordered with coloured glass – yellow, blue and purple – so that the viewer could experience the cool of winter through to the mellow hues of autumn.

Apart from William Gilpin, Romantic interpreters of the landscape of the Lakes were mainly visitors. But there was one native born literary genius who stamped his mark indelibly on the Lake District. Wordsworth's literary interest was encouraged by his father who urged him to learn Shakespeare and Milton by heart and gave him access to his library, but also bequeathed a straitened existence. John Wordsworth was legal and political agent to the 1st Earl of Lonsdale, a difficult, eccentric man who refused to pay William and his siblings the £8,000 owing at their father's death in 1783. His kinder heir finally paid up in 1802.

In 1799 William Wordsworth and his sister Dorothy set up home at Dove Cottage, just outside Grasmere. Many of William's finest poems were written there, including *The Prelude* which recalled his childhood in Cockermouth, while Dorothy composed her journal. Thereafter they never left the Lakes, moving to Rydal in 1808 and attracting other literary figures, such as Coleridge and Southey, to join them. This group is often called the School of Lake Poets, but their literary style was disparate. What linked them was their interest in landscape and their appreciation of the local community.

It would be a mistake to regard the Lakes at any time as a pastoral idyll, untouched by industry. Quarrying, mining and smelting were traditional activities since the earliest times. When Thomas Gray visited Sizergh in 1769, he saw the ancient castle, but also walked down by the river and heard the thumping of the huge hammers of the iron forge. Water was then the major source of power and had it remained so, the remoteness of the Lakes might have been overcome to establish heavy industry. That threat was removed by the development of steam, and it was Lancashire and Yorkshire that became industrial centres. Another threat took its place – the railways – and with them tourism and suburban development. In 1844 William Wordsworth led the opposition to a railway progressing beyond Windermere, writing a sonnet for the occasion asking 'Is there no nook of English ground secure/From rash assault?' – a question that is still valid today.

Wicken Fen

Wicken Fen, just seventeen miles north west of Cambridge, consists of eight hundred acres of undrained fenland, all that remains of the Fens of the Great Level that once stretched from Lincolnshire to Suffolk. Around 4,500 years ago the clay gault landscape endured a series of inundations that built up layers of vegetation and developed into peat bog. For centuries the local population exploited the natural products, digging peat for fuel and harvesting sedge for thatching and kindling. Saw sedge, *Cladium mariscus*, lives up to its name: special leather gloves were used to handle it. Cut between March and August, it was transported by barge to Ely and Cambridge.

But peat and sedge seemed small fry to agricultural improvers in the seventeenth century, and much of the Fens was drained under a series of schemes encouraged by Charles I. A Dutch engineer, Cornelis Vermuyden, built channels to carry water to the sea via the Great Ouse and the Nene. The rectangular pattern of these channels still dominates the East Anglian landscape. What Vermuyden and his fellow adventurers failed to realise was that the peat shrinks as it dries out, creating a problem for the landscape which is with us still, despite centuries of pumping to maintain levels of moisture.

The villagers of Wicken recognised that the draining was defective and sought to halt the proceedings, first by riot, then by petition. Their arguments were rejected, and Adventurers' Fen was duly drained. But Sedge Fen and others remained, divided into strips on a common rights basis. Even when all the areas around succumbed to development, the people of Wicken held out, insisting that the natural fen products were more valuable than the arable crops produced on the drained land.

Their life was a hard one, often close to subsistence level, as can be seen at Fen Cottage in Lode Lane. In the eighteenth and nineteenth centuries it represented two dwellings. The owners were totally dependent on the fen for their food, their livelihood and the fabric of their house. Fen Cottage has a chimney of brick from gault clay, walls of timber infilled with reed bundles and overlaid with clay and lime daub mixed with the sedge. Turf provided the fuel in the open hearth.

A blue-tail damsel fly at Wicken shown here at about five times its actual size.

Despite the stubbornness of the villagers at Wicken, by the mid-nineteenth century it looked as if they and their fens were doomed to extinction through the enthusiasm to drain and develop their land. But then help came from an unexpected source: the burgeoning study of entomology at Cambridge University. Drawn by the abundance and diversity of insect life, tutors brought their students out to Wicken from the 1840s, describing it as 'The Home of Ease for Entomologists'. Sedge cutters, recognising the value of the pupae of the swallowtail, soon began to offer equipment, accommodation and expert guiding to the best spots. So many oil lamps were set up to attract the insects that complaints were made that Wicken looked like a city at night.

This lucky sequence ensured Wicken's survival. When yet another threat of draining loomed in 1893, the entomologist J. C. Moberley bought up two acres of the strips that were held in common by the fenlanders, and six years later sold them to the National Trust, then a very new organisation. Wicken Fen was declared a nature reserve — the first of its kind in Britain.

Visitors to Wicken can today enjoy its very rich natural history. Successors to the Cambridge entomologists will see over 5,000 species of insect, including eighteen types of damsel and dragon flies. Butterflies include the brimstone, comma and Essex skipper. Hides have been built to observe a long list of birds from marsh harriers to bittern and owls. Litter fields, with their mixture of grasses and reed, are cut every two years for hay. This regime provides a wealth of wild flowers such as the marsh pea, yellow flag and fen violet. The sedge fields, meanwhile, are cut every three years in the traditional manner, and the sedge sold for thatching.

Wicken's precarious past can be recalled by a visit to Fen Cottage, and to the drainage wind-pump that continues to keep the water levels up and thus preserve this important wetland site, which one of the National Trust staff calls 'Britain's Rain Forest'.

Kinver Edge

Detail of some of the rock houses in the middle storey at Kinver.

The landscape often provides the materials for a home – Fen Cottage at Wicken is a good example of vernacular architecture (p.36). But it is very rare to find homes that *are* the landscape. Since Tudor times, however, people have lived in caves carved out of the red sandstone escarpment of Kinver Edge in Staffordshire. An eighteenth-century traveller was astonished to find some of these troglodytes when he stumbled upon Holy Austin Rock at the southern end of the Edge during a thunderstorm:

> I found this exceedingly curious rock inhabited by a clean and decent family, who entertained me during the violence of the tempest with what had been done, how long they had lived there, and the immense trouble they had been at in excavating the rock for their purposes. The rooms are really curious warm and commodious and the garden extremely pretty, lying on a shelve of rock towards the south.

By the early nineteenth century, when Kinver was a thriving industrial centre, eighty inhabitants occupied dwellings in Holy Austin Rock – iron-workers, agricultural workers, besom makers, and even a mole catcher. This way of life came to an end in the 1950s, when health officials began to rehouse the families in the nearby village, and in 1964 four of the derelict cottages were bought by the National Trust.

Although the dwellings were now deserted, the former way of life was pieced together with old photographs and interviews. Elisabeth Taylor had lived in a cave about halfway down Holy Austin Rock in the mid-1930s. She recalled how light and airy the houses were, warm in winter, cool in summer. The five rooms in her family house were limewashed, with quarry tile floors, fireplaces, and niches carved out of the soft red sandstone to provide cupboards and shelves. Oil and gas heated and lit the house, while hot water was on tap by way of a tank on one side of the living room grate.

After the Second World War, the rock houses of Kinver Edge attracted tourists from far and wide, who were provided with tea at 1s 6d a go. Sadly, many of the visitors to the caves after the families had moved out were vandals, and the homes fell rapidly into disrepair. Now the National Trust has rebuilt the row of houses at the summit and installed a caretaker, so that something of this extraordinary way of life can be seen again.

The Sherborne Estate

Intensive farming might seem a feature of modern times, but not so. In the late sixteenth century, 'floating' water meadows were created in England's chalk and limestone valleys. In winter, warm water, rich in nutrients, was drawn by a system of channels from the river into adjacent meadowland. A series of radiating ridges and furrows directed the water over the tops of the ridges and down the sides in continuous sheets, thus warming the cold soil and feeding it with natural fertilisers.

This ingenious system was operated by drowners, who also tended the grass and rebuilt any furrows that needed attention. In March, the sluice gates would close and the land was put over to ewes with their lambs. It has been estimated that 1 acre of land could feed 400 ewes and their offspring in one day. In April the sheep were taken off and irrigation reinstated to encourage grass. In June the hay was harvested – the first of two, or even three, crops, and then cattle brought in to graze. In November, the drowning began again.

Once a common feature of the English landscape, these meadows are now extremely rare. Another intensive system, the application of chemical fertilisers, took over in the early twentieth century. On the Sherborne Estate in Gloucestershire, the meadows fell into disuse in the 1930s, but in 1992 the National Trust decided to reinstate 140 acres (57 hectares) adjoining the River Windrush under a Countryside Stewardship scheme. With the help of the National Rivers Authority, 7 miles of channels were re-dug. Volunteers cleaned out the stone sluices, while local craftsmen rebuilt the wooden gates using oak grown on the estate.

In the years since, the Sherborne water meadows have undergone a renaissance. Despite a complete ban on chemicals and farmyard manure, the hay crop has increased and sheep and cattle flourished. A good habitat has been provided for butterflies, damsel and dragon flies, and for wading birds like the redshank, lapwing and snipe. And barn owls, vole and song thrushes – all too rare a sight – have returned to the Windrush Valley.

[42]

The Durham Coast

The coal-blackened beach at Horden with the colliery in the background; a photograph taken in 1989.

Most of the landscapes described in this book have developed gradually over the years, centuries or millennia. But landscapes are very vulnerable and can alter amazingly quickly. Nowhere is this more evident than the coast, which is why in 1965 the National Trust launched Enterprise Neptune with the long-term aim to secure 1,000 miles of coastline of outstanding beauty in England, Wales and Northern Ireland. It is the only area where the Trust *actively* campaigns to acquire property.

The halfway mark in Neptune's quest was a very interesting acquisition – the coal-blackened beach near Easington in County Durham, bought for £1 from British Coal in 1988. This coast, between the rivers Wear and Tees, has supplied coal for British households and factories for centuries – in the past hundred years from collieries that stretched for miles under the sea itself. Years of dumping the waste from the mines had covered the beaches with grime, so that J. B. Priestley in his *English Journey* written in 1933 observed 'the coast itself … has a dirty and depressing look. The sea was dingy and had somehow lost its usual adventurous escaping quality.'

Not a likely candidate for the attentions of the National Trust. But the director for this region in the 1980s, Oliver Maurice, recognised that beautiful features lurked under the grime, and that the beaches, clifftops and wooded valleys or denes contained a series of important natural habitats. Realising that the collieries were destined to close, he purchased Beacon Hill from a local farmer in 1987, and marked the 500th mile of Enterprise Neptune with the acquisition of Horden Beach. Now the Trust owns over six miles of the coast, and has spent the last ten years clearing some of rubbish that inevitably accompanies industrial activities, including two colliery heaps. But it is the sea that has displayed the most energy, removing the spoil that blackened the beach, and turning it golden with a speed that has amazed. The work continues with a Millennium project, 'Turning the Tide', where the Trust is working with other conservation bodies and local authorities to create an area that is open and accessible, and where people can enjoy the peace and natural beauty of this coastline.

Orford Ness

Sunrise at Stony Ditch Point on Orford Ness.

ஐௐ

The Suffolk coast has a mournful beauty all of its own. The bleak, uncompromising landscape inspired the work of the late eighteenth-century poet, George Crabbe, and through him Benjamin Britten's opera, *Peter Grimes*.

Stretching ten miles south of Aldeburgh is the narrow shingle spit of Orford Ness. It runs parallel with the mainland, separated from it by the River Ore, which it forces ever further south. For centuries Orford provided vital shelter from the winter storms that swept in from the North Sea, but as tidal changes caused the river to silt up and the spit to form, so the harbour lost its importance as one of the great ports of the east coast. Instead, a lighthouse was erected on the Ness itself in the sixteenth century following a stormy night when thirty-seven ships were lost. This was replaced in 1792 by the present lighthouse (Upper Light) that is still maintained by Trinity House.

In the nineteenth century the Ness was home to coastguards and lighthousemen with their families, and in summer cattle were grazed here. Its estuarial mudflats and wind ridges in the shingle provided ideal habitats for marsh birds like the avocet and the marsh harrier, and for colonies of gulls. But in the twentieth century, it took on quite a different life. The flat terrain and isolated situation proved ideal for military purposes, so it was used by the Royal Flying Corps in the First World War, with an establishment of over six hundred staff. In the 1930s trials for radar were conducted here, and in the Second World War, Barnes Wallis experimented with new types of bomb. With the Cold War aerials were established on the Cobra Mist site, providing a sophisticated defence system for gathering information world-wide. Pagodas for testing nuclear warhead detonators gave the Ness a strangely exotic skyline.

This litany of military might ended in the 1970s, when the Ministry of Defence declared Orford Ness surplus to requirements, and twenty years later the National Trust was able to buy a five-mile stretch. Once more the Ness can be an area of wilderness for the avocet and the marsh harrier, although the structures of war will remain as a sinister backdrop to the landscape.

PHOTOGRAPHS

The National Trust Photographic Library

Ian West, front cover
Charlie Waite, p.1
David Noton, p.5
Michael Caldwell, pp.7, 9
Joe Cornish, pp.11, 15, 21, 25, 33, 35, 41, 45, 47
Graeme Norways, p.13
Paul Wakefield, p.17
Matthew Antrobus, p.19
Angelo Hornak, p.27
Nick Meers, p.29
Chris King, p.31
Ray Hallett, p.37
Jonathan Player, p.39
Michael Walters, back cover

The publishers also wish to thank:
The Trustees of the National Museums & Galleries of Northern Ireland
for permission to reproduce the illustration on p.23
Country Life Photographic Library, p.43